Juan Gonzalez

JUAN GONE!

by
Evan Grant

SPORTS PUBLISHING INC.
www.SportsPublishingInc.com

Production manager: Susan M. McKinney
Cover design: Scot Muncaster
Photos: *The Associated Press* and the Texas Rangers

ISBN: 1-58261-048-7
Library of Congress Catalog Card Number: 99-61947

SPORTS PUBLISHING INC.
SportsPublishingInc.com

Printed in the United States.

CONTENTS

Juan Gonzalez, center, and teammate Ivan Rodriquez talk with Puerto Rico's first lady, Maga Nevarez de Rosello, about relief efforts after Hurricane Georges. (AP/Wide World Photos)

CHAPTER ONE

A Bold Prediction

In January of 1998, Texas Rangers manager Johnny Oates made his second trip to Vega Baja, Puerto Rico to see the little town where two of his superstars, Ivan "Pudge" Rodriguez and Juan Gonzalez, grew up.

The first time, he went with a group of Rangers officials. They were shown the nicest parts of town. The second time, he took his wife, Gloria, and traveled on his own because he wanted them both to get a sense of the different world from which the superstars came.

They got a different view all right. They saw the not-so-pretty streets of the poor town. They passed by drug deals and ramshackle homes.

From out of the bleary backdrop, an old man hurried across the street when he saw Oates wearing a Rangers hat.

"Juan Gonzalez will hit 63 home runs this year," the man said, flashing a toothless smile. "I guarantee it."

When Oates told the story, he added his own finish: "And, you know, the funny thing is, he's capable of it."

A month later, Juan Gonzalez was sitting alone in a tiny Chinese restaurant in Port Charlotte, Florida, where the Rangers hold spring training. He carefully shoveled a plate of rice into his mouth as he listened to the story.

At the end, he broke into a big smile, which slowly spread across his tanned face and curled the ends of his mustache.

The man's prediction and his manager's embellishment tickled Juan because all the pieces were in place for him to have a big season.

After a strong finish to 1997, Juan resisted the urge to play winter ball in Puerto Rico. A year earlier, he injured his thumb in winter ball and missed a month of the Rangers' season. Instead, he spent the offseason working out daily with a personal trainer. When he reported to spring training, he was the healthiest he'd ever been and in the best shape of his career, too.

That's why he smiled.

"I know the key is to stay healthy and work hard," Juan said. "The rest will take care of itself, whether my future is to hit 50 home runs or more or break a record. I know that I have the possibility to hit a lot of home runs and drive in a lot of runs, but the big thing is to stay healthy.

"When I'm healthy and positive, anything is possible. I want to play 162 games and see what happens. If I'm healthy, I have a big feeling about a big year."

The only thing Juan didn't know is just how big a year it would turn out to be.

igor the Magnificent

On October 16, 1969, the same day that the New York Mets officially became "The Amazing Mets," by completing a World Series upset of Baltimore, another amazing thing happened in Vega Baja, Puerto Rico.

Juan Alberto Gonzalez was born.

By the time he was six or seven, Juan, like most children in Puerto Rico, was playing baseball. But it wasn't like the baseball that most little leaguers in the mainland United States play. In the poor little town, the children often went without state-of-the-

Juan, now a member of the Texas Rangers, grew up in Vega Baja, Puerto Rico. (AP/Wide World Photos)

art equipment. Usually, they played in the streets. Sometimes, they played barefoot. Sometimes the bat would be a broomstick. Sometimes the ball would be a bottle cap or, as Gonzalez once said, "the head off one of my sister's dolls."

Other things went on in the streets of Vega Baja, too. As Juan grew up, Alto de Cuba, the barrio or neighborhood in which he grew up, turned increasingly tough. Drug deals took place, as well as other crimes.

His father, Juan Sr., was worried about what might happen if his family stayed in the barrio. So, when young Juan was 12, the Gonzalez family moved.

"I had a good home where morals played a very important role," Juan once said. "My parents taught me that you can get ahead in life if you do honest work. You'll live a good life."

For Juan, the good life meant baseball, though like other children his interests were varied. Always taller than his classmates, Juan enjoyed basketball and volleyball, too. And he had a particular fondness for professional wrestling, especially a character named "The Mighty Igor." Juan pretended to be Igor and called himself "Igor the Great." The nickname stuck. Even today, his closest friends still call him Igor.

About the same time, though, Juan started to make his given name known, too, as a legitimate baseball prospect.

He was already about a head taller than most of the kids he played with. And by the time, he was 13 the legend of Juan Gonzalez was already being born. He was already starting to catch the eyes of major league scouts, who came to Puerto Rico to find diamonds in the rough.

At the time, players in Puerto Rico were not subject to major league baseball's amateur draft. As long as they were 16, or could provide a piece of paper that said they were, they could negotiate with any team that was interested.

Juan's power and his strong throwing arm drew a lot of interest. According to one story, he hit three home runs in a game. It wasn't too long after that the scouts started showing up at his games and his home trying to persuade him that their team offered him the quickest route to the majors and the best chance at a World Championship.

The Yankees stopped by. So did the Toronto Blue Jays. And the California Angels, Chicago White Sox and Texas Rangers, too.

What ensued was a bidding war the likes of which Puerto Rico had never seen before. In the end, the Rangers and Blue Jays were the two teams left standing.

The Blue Jays were the defending champions of the American League East. The Rangers were usually a losing team. Juan figured his quickest path to the majors was to go with the team that needed the most help. So, on May 30, 1986, nearly six months before his 17th birthday, Juan accepted the Rangers' offer of a $75,000 signing bonus. At the time, it was the highest bonus ever paid to a Puerto Rican player.

But according to Luis Rosa, the scout who signed him, it was money well-spent.

"Let me assure you," Rosa said after Juan signed, "Juan Gonzalez is the finest prospect to come out of Puerto Rico in years."

Juan was on his way.

CHAPTER THREE

An Enduring Friendship

In June of 1986 on a steamy Florida field, two thin, exceptionally talented teenaged outfielders met for the first time. They had little in common except that they were both superb baseball talents and neither spoke a word of English.

From those humble beginnings, Juan and the kid from the Dominican Republic, Sammy Sosa, forged a friendship that is still strong today.

They both wanted to reach the major leagues. Once there, they wanted to make big impacts. And both wanted to give something back. That was a

***Juan and Sammy Sosa (above) who also began his
professional baseball career with the Texas Rangers,
remain close friends.(Ron Vesely)***

long way away, though. In 1986 Juan and Sammy were just beginning their pro careers with Sarasota of the Gulf Coast League, the bottom rung on the minor league ladder. At that point, the grand plan was more a dream than a blueprint.

"We had the same dreams," Juan said.

They also had incredible talent. Even then, long before the teenagers completely filled out, it was easily recognizable.

Their statistics for that first season weren't amazing. Juan hit .240 without even one home run and just 36 runs batted in. Sammy didn't do much better. He hit .275 with four home runs and 28 RBIs.

That didn't stop Omar Minaya, who was a Rangers scout in Latin American and later a coach with that Sarasota team, from filing glowing scouting reports on the pair at the end of the season.

"Sammy is a kid who possesses a lot of potential," Minaya wrote. "He is very aggressive and wishes to play in the major leagues very badly. . . . Most people love his personality and he is a pleasure to watch playing."

Of Juan, Minaya proved just to be just as prophetic.

"Juan possesses a good body that should develop nicely. His two most impressive qualities are the way in which the ball jumps off his bat and his feel for the RBI. . . . He should go to a league where he can hit home runs."

One thing stuck in Minaya's mind: Juan's ability to drive in runs. He remembered the first game he saw the skinny outfielder play for Sarasota. Sammy had reached base earlier in the inning and stolen second. But when Juan reached the plate there were two outs and he quickly fell behind in the count, 0-and-2.

"He's battling this 22-year-old pitcher," Minaya said. "He's fouling balls off, fouling balls off. And we notice one thing about him—he choked up on the bat a little. He knew the situation was an RBI situation. He hit a single right up the middle. And I remember Sandy Johnson [who was the Rangers' scouting director] saying at that moment, 'This kid will always drive in runs.'"

In 1987, the dynamic duo stepped up a level to Gastonia (North Carolina). Juan finally hit his first home run and then 13 more. He drove in 74 runs. He was named to the South Atlantic League All-Star. Sammy hit 11 homers.

The next year they went to the Florida State League, the next step up, and continued impressing people even though neither of them had as many as 10 home runs.

"[Juan] was a beautiful kid," said Montreal manager Felipe Alou, who managed in the minors

Juan has been with the Texas Rangers organization since signing his first professional contract at the age of 16. (Texas Rangers)

at the time. "He had long legs, strides, all of that stuff. He was not a power hitter then, but at that point you don't care about stats."

The next year, when they both moved up to Class AA, everybody started caring. Sammy hit nearly .300 for the first half of the season and when the Rangers needed an emergency outfielder to replace injured Pete Incaviglia, they called Sammy.

"I'll see you in 15 days," Juan said.

"No, no, no," Sammy said. "You aren't going to see me here anymore."

He was right. Just a month into Sammy's major league career, the Rangers found themselves on the fringes of a pennant race. They needed a veteran hitter to push them toward the team's first playoff appearance. The Chicago White Sox wanted Sammy in return. On July 30, Sammy and pitcher Wilson Alvarez went to Chicago in a trade for Harold Baines and infielder Fred Manrique. Juan and Sammy would never get the chance to play in the Rangers outfield together.

Juan, however, wasn't far behind. The Rangers called him up in September when major league teams look at their top minor league prospects. He even hit his first major league home run.

He started 1990 with Oklahoma City, in Class AAA, the step just below the majors. He tore up the Pacific Coast League, hitting 29 homers and driving in 101 runs. In September, six weeks before he turned 21, he received another callup to the majors.

This time, he wouldn't be going back.

Sammy and Juan had both realized their dream. They both were major leaguers. It was, however, only the start of the dream.

C H A P T E R   F O U R

The New Clemente

Boys who grew up in Puerto Rico in the 1960s and 1970s loved two things: Baseball and Roberto Clemente.

Actually for a lot of Puerto Ricans, Clemente and baseball are one and the same.

Clemente was born in Carolina, Puerto Rico in 1934 and reached the major leagues in 1955 with Pittsburgh, the team for which he played all of his 18-year career. He eventually became one of the greatest right fielders in the history of the game and along with it captured the hearts of the entire is-

Roberto Clemente remains one of Puerto Rico's national heroes. (Pittsburgh Pirates)

land. In the last week of the 1972 season, Clemente reached 3,000 hits, becoming the first Latin American player to reach that plateau.

But Clemente was more than just a great player. He was devoted to Puerto Rico and the entire Latin American community. When a devastating earthquake rocked Managua, Nicaragua in December of 1972, Clemente helped lead relief efforts. Then he accompanied the plane carrying the supplies to Managua. The plane, however, developed trouble and crashed in the Caribbean Sea on New Year's Eve. Clemente's body was never found.

The entire island mourned for years. Even today, Clemente's name is synonymous with sports. One of the island's major sports training facilities is called *Ciudad Deportiva Roberto Clemente* or Roberto Clemente City. Also, the major coliseum on the island is named for Clemente.

ROBERTO WALKER CLEMENTE
PITTSBURGH N. L. 1955-1972
MEMBER OF EXCLUSIVE 3,000-HIT CLUB. LED
NATIONAL LEAGUE IN BATTING FOUR TIMES.
HAD FOUR SEASONS WITH 200 OR MORE HITS
WHILE POSTING LIFETIME .317 AVERAGE AND
240 HOME RUNS. WON MOST VALUABLE PLAYER
AWARD 1966. RIFLE-ARMED DEFENSIVE STAR
SET N. L. MARK BY PACING OUTFIELDERS IN
ASSISTS FIVE YEARS. BATTED .362 IN TWO
WORLD SERIES, HITTING IN ALL 14 GAMES.

After being killed in a plane crash during a relief effort to Nicaragua, Clemente was inducted into the Baseball Hall of Fame just six months after his death. (Baseball Hall of Fame)

But while the island had plenty of memories, it had no successor to Clemente, who was named to the baseball Hall of Fame just six months after his death, as a national hero.

"For years, we had nothing," said former major leaguer Ivan DeJesus. "Then Clemente, then nothing. Now, we have Juan."

Juan quickly ascended to the rank of national hero for two reasons. First, he quickly became one of the top power hitters in the major leagues. Second, he never forgot the people, especially the needy, of his beloved Puerto Rico.

In 1992, only his second full season in the major leagues, Juan hit 43 home runs, the most in all of baseball. It was the first time since Orlando Cepeda did it more than 30 years earlier that a Latin American player led one of the major leagues in homers. And Juan was only 22 years old. Only five men had ever led the major leagues at a younger age and all of them were in the Hall of Fame.

Juan, center, with shortstop Domingo Cedeno, left, and second baseman Luis Alicea. (AP/Wide World Photos)

When Juan returned home after the season, he was treated like a conquering hero. A crowd of 5,000 people was at the airport to greet him. A motorcade of 15 police cars escorted him the 23 miles to Vega Baja and another 100,000 people showed up along the way to wave to him. And another 3,000 were waiting in Vega Baja's main plaza. Juan cried at the reception.

Only then did his real contributions start. He played in the Puerto Rico Winter League that year and his presence helped save the once-proud league from drowning financially. He visited schools all over the island. Everywhere he went, the crowds followed.

"When my playing days are over, I will be focused on serving the people of Puerto Rico, not from a political platform, but from a social platform," Juan told a visiting reporter that winter. "God gave me a good mind and the ability to succeed in baseball. I understand that I have to give back for what God has given me."

The next year, Juan outdid himself. He hit 46 home runs to lead the American League again and tie for the major league lead. At the time, only 10 other men in history had led the majors in homers in consecutive years and some of them were named Babe Ruth, Ted Williams and Jimmie Foxx—three of the greatest home run hitters of all time.

But he did more than that. He hit .310, proving he was dangerous as more than just a home run hitter. He also drove in 118 runs, his second straight year with more than 100 RBIs.

When he returned home to Puerto Rico, the tumultuous welcome started all over again.

Juan was not the first player to be hailed as the "next Clemente," only the one who seemed to be most up to carrying on the spirit of the island's enduring hero.

Other players had tried. But either their production diminished or their reputations were tarnished by messy incidents in their private lives.

"There's a lot of pressure on me," Juan said. "That's OK. I understand it. It's what I have to do for my people. Everybody knows what I can do between the lines. I have to do things outside the lines. I want my people to be proud of me. They need somebody."

According to those who know Juan, he is that somebody.

"He's always done better than anyone before or after Clemente when it comes to giving to the people," said Juan's friend Luis Mayoral, who broadcasts Rangers games in Spanish. "Juan's always had that natural desire to be like that. I think Juan would tell you that Clemente is in a class by himself, but he's proud to follow in his footsteps."

Puerto Rico had a new hero.

Juan led the American League in home runs in 1992 and 1993. (Texas Rangers)

Trouble in Paradise

As 1993 faded into 1994, things couldn't have looked better for Juan.

He was the two-time defending AL home run champion. He wasn't 25 years old and he had already hit 121 home runs, an average of about 40 per season. If he kept that up over a 15-year career or longer, he stood an excellent chance of threatening Henry Aaron's all-time record of 755 home runs. He had received a new contract that could be worth as much as $45 million over seven years.

Life, it seemed, was wonderful.

At the end of the 1993 season, everything seemed to be going Juan's way. (AP/Wide World Photos)

But things aren't always what they seem.

The 1994 season was to be one of the most forgettable in baseball history. It was shortened by a bitter strike between the players and owners. No player would like to forget about 1994 more than Juan.

The first signs of trouble started even before spring training. The Rangers had planned to honor Juan as the team's Player of the Year at their annual winter banquet. It was supposed to be his first public appearance after signing the new contract. But Juan never made it to the banquet. He miscalculated the amount of time it took to drive to the airport and missed the flight from Puerto Rico.

It was only the start of a slew of bad news. During the first week of the season, Juan married his girlfriend, Elaine Lopez. The couple didn't live together for more than a month, but a bitter feud developed between the two families. It culminated when several members of the Lopez family showed up at a Kansas City hotel wanting to confront Juan.

Though the confrontation never took place, the trouble in his personal life apparently carried over to Juan's performance on the field. In the previous two seasons, Juan averaged a home run every 12.5 at-bats. During one stretch in 1994, Juan went 99 at-bats without a home run.

When the strike finally brought the baseball season to a halt in August, Juan had just 19 home runs and 85 RBIs. Not only did the defending AL home run champ fail to keep his title, he finished out of the top 10. He was tied for 20th in the AL.

The poor season, the strike and the public marital problems had affected Juan's reputation at home, too. When he played winter ball in Puerto Rico, he was often booed on the road.

"I'm sorry this happened, because Juan has done so many things for the island," said Sixto

Lezcano, a former major leaguer who was Juan's winter league manager. "But he's a public figure and everybody looks at him. Everyone has trouble in their youth. The good thing is Juan could come out of it better if he learns from it."

Juan put most of the personal problems behind him after 1994, but 1995, which got off to a late start because the strike lingered through March, proved to be just as rough on the field. First, Juan showed up at spring training with more muscle on his 6-foot-3 frame than ever before. In football that might be a good thing. In baseball, bulk tends to get in the way of a power hitter's swing. Extra muscle also can make baseball players more brittle and more susceptible to injuries. That's exactly what happened to Juan in 1995.

In the middle of spring training, he bent down to tie his shoe and felt a twinge in his back. The twinge turned out to be a herniated disc that forced him to miss the first month of the season. Later, sore legs knocked him out of the lineup for nearly a week. Juan missed three more weeks with a neck injury.

At the end of the season, he had hit only 27 home runs and driven in just 82 runs—a career low in RBIs.

"This winter I'm going to work hard to get back in shape," Juan said as the season wound down. "I like being in Texas and I want to stay here. I feel good. My personal problems are behind me. Right now, everything is in control."

Juan made a vow at the end of the season: He intended to come back better than ever in 1996.

CHAPTER SIX

Finding the Way Home

Going into the 1996 season, perhaps no organization knew futility better than the Texas Rangers.

The Rangers were originally born in 1961 as the Washington Senators. That franchise's lack of success and the poor attendance it generated helped move the franchise west to Texas in 1972. Aside from the occasional winning season, the Rangers hadn't fared much better in their new home. Going into their 25th season in Texas, they still had never been to the playoffs. No other team in the majors had as long a drought.

In 1996, Juan had five home runs and 25 RBIs in April. (Texas Rangers)

The 1996 Rangers were determined to finally end the dry spell. And having a healthy, productive Juan Gonzalez was an important part of that plan.

Juan showed up at spring training early. When he arrived, he had dropped nearly 20 pounds, just as the Rangers had asked. He also agreed to move from left field to right field, a position he had never played before. Juan worked hard at the position change, learning to play the different angles in right field.

The season couldn't have started better for the Rangers. They won their first seven games. Juan started out hot, too. He had a four RBIs in third game of the season and six in a game two weeks later. At the end of April, the Rangers were in first place and Juan was hitting .299 with five home runs and 25 RBIs.

Then an old problem arose. On May 7, Juan suffered a torn quadriceps muscle in his left leg and

Juan uses a mirror to practice his swing. (AP/Wide World Photos)

had to go on the disabled list for the third time in less than two seasons. It would cost him three weeks of the season.

In the past, the injury might have cost him more time, but Juan started working with a new personal trainer, Angel "Nao" [pronounced Now] Precinal and found himself ready to return to the lineup in three weeks, though he had to split time between right field and designated hitter. His bat, though, was completely healthy. It showed.

He hit .315 in June with 11 home runs and 27 RBIs. And that was only the warm-up act. In July, he hit 15 home runs—tying the major league record for the most home runs hit in that month—and he set a team record with 38 RBIs. He also hit .407 and was named the AL's Player of the Month.

"It was an amazing streak," said Rangers long-time broadcaster Eric Nadel. "He was an RBI machine. He almost single-handedly kept the Rangers in first place."

The offensive outburst didn't stop there. In August, he hit .311 with nine more homers and 28 RBIs. He entered on the verge of doing things he'd never done before. His 41 home runs were just five shy of the club record he set in 1993. His 123 RBIs were already a club record.

The Rangers were on the verge of doing something historic, too. They entered September in first place.

Though the team—and Juan—slumped a bit in September, the Rangers clinched their first AL West title in the last week of the season. Juan hit his 47th homer, breaking the club record, in the final week. He finished with 144 RBIs.

The most amazing exhibition was still to come. In the playoffs, the Rangers traveled to New York to face the Yankees, champions of the AL East.

In the first playoff game in franchise history, the Rangers fell behind 1-0, but in the fourth inning, Juan hit a three-run homer off David Cone to give the Rangers the lead. They held on to win 6-2.

Juan homered twice in Game 2, but the Rangers lost in 12 innings. In Game 3, the first postseason game played in Texas, Juan homered in the fourth inning to tie the score at one. The Rangers eventually took a 2-1 lead, but the Yankees scored twice in the ninth to win, 3-2.

Facing elimination, the Rangers turned to Juan again. He homered in the third to give the Rangers a 4-0 lead. Again, though, it wasn't enough. The Rangers didn't score again and the Yankees, who went on to win the World Series, rallied for six runs.

When the dust from the playoffs had finally cleared, Juan had an unbelievable .438 average. He hit five homers and drove in nine runs.

During the 1996 playoffs, Juan batted .438 with five home runs and nine RBI. (AP/Wide World Photos)

A month later, the finishing touches were put on Juan's amazing season. He was named the AL's Most Valuable Player.

Juan was back on top.

Juan is popular with fans in Texas as well as Puerto Rico. (AP/Wide World Photos)

A Monster Year

No sooner had Juan regained his place as one of the best players in baseball than the old troubles surfaced again.

His MVP award restored him to hero status in the hearts of Puerto Rican fans. They all but demanded that he play in the winter league. Despite playing 134 games during the regular season and the playoffs, Juan wanted to give something back to the baseball fans at home. So, after a year away from the winter league, he returned. The Rangers weren't in favor of the idea because it created more possibility for an injury.

Unfortunately for Juan, that's exactly what happened. On the final day of the winter league season, he dove for a ball in the outfield and bent his thumb backwards. He felt something pop. He had torn a ligament and needed surgery. Even worse, he was probably going to miss at least the first six months of the season.

Juan vowed then never to play winter ball again. He also made another promise:

"I'll be back sooner than they say," he said.

He did make it back earlier, joining the team on May 1 and missing just four weeks. Once back, he was the Juan of 1996. The Rangers, however, weren't.

Though Juan hit 42 homers—his fourth season with 40 or more homers—and drove in 131 runs, it wasn't enough. There were too many other injuries on the team and the Rangers couldn't repeat as AL West champions.

Juan promised bigger things in 1998.

He spent all winter working with Angel Precinal, making his body more limber and more resistant to injury. He arrived at the Rangers' spring training camp in Port Charlotte, Florida, early. Everywhere he went, people predicted big things for him.

"The possibilities for him are limitless," said Minnesota pitcher Bob Tewksbury, who was Juan's teammate in 1995. "He's matured to a point where a lot of things have fallen in place for him. If he's healthy, he's going to do his damage. I'm not a big predictions guy, but it's unlimited what he can do."

"I think he wants to show people that the Juan Gonzalez people might have seen in 1994 or 1995 isn't the real Juan Gonzalez," Rangers general manager Doug Melvin said. "This is the real Juan Gonzalez."

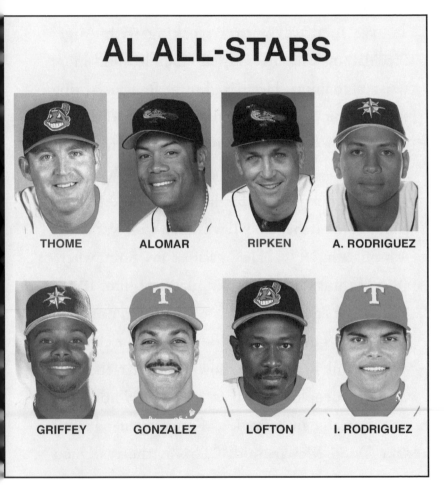

AL ALL-STARS

THOME   ALOMAR   RIPKEN   A. RODRIGUEZ

GRIFFEY   GONZALEZ   LOFTON   I. RODRIGUEZ

Juan was a member of the 1998 American League All-Star team. (AP/Wide World Photos)

While others talked about Juan chasing Roger Maris' single-season record of 61 home runs or Hack Wilson's record of 190 RBIs, Juan thought of only one number: 162. That's the number of games in a full major league season and after being on the disabled list in each of the last three seasons and having 1994 short-circuited by the strike, he wanted to be available for all of them.

"I know I have the possibility to hit a lot of home runs and drive in a lot of runs, but I have to be healthy to help my team," Juan said. "This year, I'm positive and I'm 100 percent healthy."

From opening day, the onslaught began. It started with a trickle, a single RBI in a Rangers loss in the opener. In the next game, Juan hit a grand slam and drove in four runs. By the end of April, he had 36 RBIs in just 26 games. It was the most ever by a player in the season's first month.

Juan meets the Reverend Jesse Jackson at the League of United Latin American Citizens Conference in 1998. (AP/Wide World Photos)

It continued in May with another 35 RBIs in 28 games. Through the first two months of the season, Juan had 18 homers and 70 RBIs and—perhaps more importantly—he had played in each of the Rangers' 54 games.

Slowly people around baseball began to wonder if two long-standing records were in danger. In St. Louis, Mark McGwire was taking aim at Maris' homer record, which had stood for 36 years. In Arlington, Texas, Juan was on pace to break Wilson's RBI record, which had stood since 1930.

He slowed down a bit in June, but was still averaging more than an RBI a game when he was named to the AL All-Star team for the first time since 1993. On the day before the All-Star break, Juan hit two homers and drove in four runs against Seattle's Randy Johnson. He headed to the All-Star game with 101 RBIs in 87 games.

"When Juan hits, the ball just sounds different," Rangers designated hitter Lee Stevens said. "We could take the exact same swing at the exact same pitch and it wouldn't sound the same as when Juan hits it."

In late July some back stiffness forced Juan out of the lineup for several games, but not to the disabled list. He also fell irreversibly off Wilson's pace.

Juan shrugged at losing two goals in one week. There was still something more important to be won—the AL West.

In August and September, with the Rangers trailing Anaheim, Juan led the offensive charge. He batted .368 with 14 home runs and 41 RBIs.

In late September, as the Rangers were on their way to catching and passing Anaheim for their second AL West title in three years, Juan hit the 300th home run of his career.

At the season's end, Juan had hit a career best .318. He hit 45 homers, making him one of only

12 players in history to hit 40 or more homers in a season at least five times. He led the AL with 50 doubles and 157 RBIs.

They were amazing numbers, but as soon as the regular season was done the Rangers faced a Herculean task. They had to face the New York Yankees in the playoffs. The same Yankees who knocked the Rangers out of the playoffs in 1996 were even better in 1998, winning 114 games in the regular season. That total was second in baseball history only to the 1906 Cubs.

The Yankees, who went on to win the World Series, dominated the series, allowing the Rangers' just one run in a three-game sweep.

Just like that, Juan's amazing season was over.

Or was it?

Together Again

As soon as the season ended, much like his hero, Roberto Clemente, Juan jumped in to help the less fortunate.

During late September, Puerto Rico was hit hard by Hurricane Georges and many on the island were without food or homes.

Juan helped coordinate some of the relief efforts and donated $25,000 of his own money.

"There are a lot of people suffering there," he said. "These are my people. I have a very special place in my heart for them and want to make sure they do not suffer."

Juan, shown here before a press conference in Puerto Rico, has won the American League MVP award twice in the last three seasons. (AP/Wide World Photos)

In 1998, Juan became the first Latin American baseball player to win two MVP awards. (Texas Rangers)

It was just the start of a busy offseason for him, though. A month later, his big season culminated with his second MVP award. He became the first Latin American player to win two MVPs.

What made the award all the more special was that his long-time friend and former teammate, Sammy Sosa, captured the NL award. They became the first Latin players to win the award in the same year. Though separated for nine years, they were together again.

"It's very special," Juan said. "Sammy is my friend. I was happy to see him win it. I wanted him to win it. This is a special moment for all of Latin America and all of baseball, too."

And still Juan's big year wasn't done. In December, he capped it off by marrying his long-time girlfriend Olga Tanon, a famous *merengue* singer in Puerto Rico.

Juan called 1998 the best year of his career. (AP/Wide World Photos)

Juan ended 1998 happy, healthy and successful like never before.

"This is the best year of my career," he said. "Everything in my life is just coming together. It feels wonderful."

Juan Gonzalez Quick Facts

Full Name: Juan Alberto Gonzalez

Team: Texas Rangers

Hometown: Vega Baja, Puerto Rico

Position: Outfielder

Jersey Number: 19

Bats: Right

Throws: Right

Height: 6-3

Weight: 235 pounds

Birthdate: October 16, 1969

1998 Highlight: Named American League's Most
Valuable Player

Juan has 947 career RBIs. (Texas Rangers)

Juan Gonzalez's Professional Career

Year	Club	AVG	G	AB	R	H	2B	3B	HR	RBI	BB	SO	SB
1986	Sarasota	.240	60	233*	24	56	4	1	0	36	21	57	7
1987	Gastonia	.265	127	509	69	135	21	2	14	74	30	92	9
1988	Charlotte	.256	77	277	25	71	14	3	8	43	25	64	5
1989	Tulsa	.293	133	502	73	147	30	7	21	85	31	98	1
	Texas	.150	24	60	6	9	3	0	1	7	6	17	0
1990	Oklahoma City	.258	128	496	78	128	29	4	29*	101*	32	109	2
	Texas	.289	25	90	11	26	7	1	4	12	2	18	0
1991	Texas	.264	142	545	78	144	34	1	27	102	42	118	4
1992	Texas	.260	155	584	77	152	24	2	43*	109	35	143	0
1993	Texas	.310	140	536	105	166	33	1	46*	118	37	99	4
1994	Texas	.275	107	422	57	116	18	4	19	85	30	66	6
1995	Texas	.295	90	352	57	104	20	2	27	82	17	66	0
1996	Texas	.314	134	541	89	170	33	2	47	144	45	82	2
1997	Texas	.296	133	533	87	158	24	3	42	131	33	107	0
1998	Texas	.318	154	606	110	193	50*	2	45	157*	46	126	2

M.L./Texas Totals .290 1104 4269 677 1238 246 18 301 947 293 842 18

*Led League   #Tied for League Lead

Active Career Home Run Leaders

1.	Mark McGwire	457
2.	Barry Bonds	411
3.	Jose Canseco	397
4.	Cal Ripken	384
5.	Fred McGriff	358
6.	Gary Gaetti	351
7.	Ken Griffey Jr.	350
8.	Harold Baines	348
9.	Darryl Strawberry	332
10.	Andres Galarraga	332
11.	Chili Davis	331
12.	Albert Belle	321
13.	Cecil Fielder	319
14.	Rafael Palmeiro	314
15.	**Juan Gonzalez**	**301**

In 1998, Juan batted .318 with 45 home runs and a league-leading 157 RBI. (AP/Wide World Photos)

Active Career Slugging Percentage

1.	Frank Thomas	.584
2.	Albert Belle	.577
3.	Mark McGwire	.576
4.	Mike Piazza	.575
5.	Ken Griffey Jr.	.568
6.	**Juan Gonzalez**	**.568**
7.	Manny Ramirez	.558
8.	Barry Bonds	.556
9.	Nomar Garciaparra	.552
	Larry Walker	.552
10.	Jim Thome	.549

AL MVP Winners in the '90s

1998   Juan Gonzalez, Texas

1997   Ken Griffey Jr., Seattle

1996   Juan Gonzalez, Texas

1995   Mo Vaughn, Boston

1994   Frank Thomas, Chicago

1993   Frank Thomas, Chicago

1992   Dennis Eckersley, Oakland

1991   Cal Ripken, Baltimore

1990   Rickey Henderson, Oakland

1998 AL MVP Voting

Player, Team	1st	2nd	3rd	Points
Juan Gonzalez, Texas	**21**	**7**	**—**	**357**
Nomar Garciaparra, Boston	5	7	7	232
Derek Jeter, New York	2	6	1	180
Mo Vaughn, Boston	—	3	1	135
Ken Griffey Jr., Seattle	—	—	4	135
Manny Ramirez, Cleveland	—	1	3	127
Bernie Williams, New York	—	1	3	103
Albert Belle, Chicago	—	—	4	96
Alex Rodriguez, Seattle	—	2	1	92

Juan was fourth in the American League in home runs in 1998. (AP/Wide World Photos)

1998 American League HR Leaders

Ken Griffey Jr.	56
Albert Belle	49
Jose Canseco	46
Juan Gonzalez	**45**
Manny Ramirez	45

Active Career At Bats per Home Runs

Mark McGwire	11.2
Juan Gonzalez	**14.2**
Albert Belle	14.6
Ken Griffey Jr.	14.9
Jose Canseco	15.2

1998 American League RBI Leaders

Juan Gonzalez	**157**
Albert Belle	152
Ken Griffey Jr.	146
Manny Ramirez	145
Alex Rodriguez	124

Active Career At Bats per RBI

Juan Gonzalez	**4.5**
Mark McGwire	4.5
Frank Thomas	4.6
Albert Belle	4.6
Mike Piazza	4.8

1998 American League Batting Average Leaders

Bernie Williams	.339
Mo Vaughn	.337
Albert Belle	.328
Eric Davis	.327
Derek Jeter	.324
Nomar Garciaparra	.323
Edgar Martinez	.322
Ivan Rodriguez	.321
Tony Fernandez	.321
Juan Gonzalez	**.318**

Game by Game with Juan Gonzalez in 1998

Following is a regular-season game-by-game breakdown of Juan Gonzalez' 1998 campaign, a season in which he was named the American League's Most Valuable Player.

Date	Opp	AB	R	H	2B	3B	HR	RBI
3/31/98	ChA	4	1	1	0	0	0	1
4/02/98	ChA	5	2	3	0	0	1	4
4/03/98	@Tor	5	0	3	2	0	0	1
4/04/98	@Tor	4	1	1	0	0	1	2
4/05/98	@Tor	4	1	2	1	0	0	1

Date	Opp	AB	R	H	2B	3B	HR	RBI
4/06/98	@ChA	4	0	0	0	0	0	1
4/09/98	@ChA	4	0	1	1	0	0	2
4/10/98	TOR	4	0	1	0	0	0	0
4/11/98	TOR	4	0	2	1	0	0	1
4/12/98	TOR	4	0	0	0	0	0	0
4/13/98	DET	5	1	3	0	0	1	3
4/14/98	DET	5	1	2	1	0	0	0
4/15/98	DET	4	2	2	1	0	0	1
4/17/98	BAL	5	1	3	0	0	0	1
4/18/98	BAL	4	1	2	1	0	0	0

Date	Opp	AB	R	H	2B	3B	HR	RBI
4/19/98	BAL	4	2	2	0	0	1	4
4/21/98	TB	4	0	0	0	0	0	0
4/22/98	TB	4	1	1	0	0	0	1
4/23/98	TB	4	1	1	0	0	0	0
4/24/98	@KC	5	1	1	1	0	0	1
4/25/98	@KC	4	1	3	1	0	0	5
4/26/98	@KC	5	3	3	0	0	2	4
4/27/98	@Min	3	1	0	0	0	0	1
4/28/98	@Min	5	1	2	0	0	1	2
4/29/98	@Det	4	0	0	0	0	0	0

Date	Opp	AB	R	H	2B	3B	HR	RBI
4/30/98	@Det	4	0	0	0	0	0	0
5/01/98	@Bos	4	0	0	0	0	0	0
5/02/98	@Bos	4	0	1	0	0	0	0
5/03/98	@Bos	4	0	1	0	0	0	0
5/05/98	NYA	4	0	1	0	0	0	0
5/06/98	NYA	5	3	3	0	0	1	5
5/07/98	CLE	3	1	0	0	0	0	0
5/08/98	CLE	4	1	1	1	0	0	1
5/09/98	CLE	4	1	2	0	0	1	3
5/10/98	CLE	4	0	2	1	0	0	1

Date	Opp	AB	R	H	2B	3B	HR	RBI
5/11/98	BOS	4	0	1	1	0	0	2
5/12/98	BOS	3	1	0	0	0	0	0
5/13/98	@NYA	4	2	2	1	0	1	1
5/14/98	@NYA	7	1	1	1	0	0	0
5/15/98	@Cle	6	0	0	0	0	0	1
5/16/98	@Cle	3	0	0	0	0	0	0
5/17/98	@Cle	3	0	1	0	0	0	0
5/19/98	SEA	2	1	1	0	0	0	0
5/20/98	SEA	4	0	1	1	0	0	1
5/21/98	SEA	5	2	2	1	0	1	3

Date	Opp	AB	R	H	2B	3B	HR	RBI
5/22/98	KC	4	1	2	0	0	1	5
5/23/98	KC	3	0	1	0	0	0	0
5/24/98	KC	4	1	1	0	0	1	2
5/25/98	MIN	3	0	0	0	0	0	0
5/27/98	MIN	5	0	2	1	0	0	1
5/28/98	@Bal	4	0	0	0	0	0	0
5/29/98	@Bal	4	0	1	0	0	0	0
5/30/98	@Bal	5	3	3	0	0	2	4
5/31/98	@Bal	5	2	2	0	0	2	5
6/01/98	@TB	4	0	0	0	0	0	1

Date	Opp	AB	R	H	2B	3B	HR	RBI
6/02/98	@TB	5	0	0	0	0	0	0
6/03/98	@Oak	5	1	1	0	0	1	1
6/04/98	@Oak	4	0	0	0	0	0	0
6/05/98	SD	3	1	2	1	0	1	3
6/06/98	SD	3	0	1	1	0	0	0
6/07/98	SD	2	1	1	0	0	0	1
6/08/98	@Col	4	0	0	0	0	0	0
6/09/98	@Col	4	1	2	0	0	1	1
6/10/98	@Col	5	1	2	0	0	1	2
6/12/98	ANA	4	0	2	1	0	0	0

Date	Opp	AB	R	H	2B	3B	HR	RBI
6/13/98	ANA	4	0	1	0	0	0	0
6/14/98	ANA	4	0	1	0	0	0	0
6/15/98	ANA	3	0	0	0	0	0	1
6/16/98	OAK	5	1	1	0	0	0	0
6/17/98	OAK	3	0	0	0	0	0	0
6/18/98	OAK	2	0	1	0	0	0	0
6/19/98	@Ana	4	2	3	1	0	1	5
6/20/98	@Ana	3	1	1	0	0	1	2
6/21/98	@Ana	4	1	1	0	0	0	1
6/22/98	ARI	4	0	0	0	0	0	0

Date	Opp	AB	R	H	2B	3B	HR	RBI
6/23/98	ARI	4	1	1	1	0	0	2
6/24/98	@Ari	4	0	2	0	1	0	2
6/25/98	@Ari	5	3	2	0	0	0	1
6/26/98	@SF	5	1	1	0	0	1	2
6/27/98	@SF	5	1	1	0	0	0	0
6/28/98	@SF	3	0	0	0	0	0	0
6/30/98	LA	4	0	1	1	0	0	0
7/01/98	LA	3	0	0	0	0	0	0
7/02/98	LA	4	0	1	0	0	0	0
7/03/98	SEA	4	0	1	0	0	0	0

Date	Opp	AB	R	H	2B	3B	HR	RBI
7/04/98	SEA	2	1	0	0	0	0	1
7/05/98	SEA	4	2	2	0	0	2	4
7/09/98	@Oak	4	0	0	0	0	0	0
7/10/98	@Oak	4	1	1	1	0	0	0
7/11/98	@Oak	3	0	1	1	0	0	0
7/12/98	@Oak	4	0	1	1	0	0	0
7/13/98	@Sea	4	0	2	1	0	0	0
7/14/98	@Sea	4	0	1	0	0	0	0
7/15/98	BAL	4	1	2	0	0	0	0
7/16/98	BAL	4	0	1	0	0	0	0

Date	Opp	AB	R	H	2B	3B	HR	RBI
7/17/98	TB	2	1	1	0	0	0	0
7/18/98	TB	5	2	2	2	0	0	2
7/19/98	TB	4	1	1	0	0	1	2
7/21/98	@KC	5	3	3	0	0	2	5
7/22/98	@KC	4	1	1	0	0	1	3
7/23/98	@KC	3	0	1	0	0	0	1
7/24/98	@Min	3	0	0	0	0	0	0
7/25/98	@Min	3	1	0	0	0	0	0
7/26/98	@Min	4	1	2	0	0	1	2
7/30/98	@Tor	1	0	0	0	0	0	0

Date	Opp	AB	R	H	2B	3B	HR	RBI
8/04/98	TOR	4	1	1	1	0	0	0
8/05/98	TOR	4	1	1	0	0	1	1
8/06/98	BOS	3	2	2	1	0	1	1
8/07/98	BOS	3	0	1	0	0	0	1
8/08/98	BOS	3	0	0	0	0	0	0
8/13/98	@NYA	3	0	0	0	0	0	0
8/14/98	@NYA	3	0	0	0	0	0	0
8/15/98	@NYA	4	1	1	0	0	0	0
8/16/98	@NYA	4	0	2	1	0	0	0
8/18/98	@Bos	4	1	1	0	0	1	1

Date	Opp	AB	R	H	2B	3B	HR	RBI
8/18/98	@Bos	4	1	3	0	0	0	0
8/19/98	CLE	4	0	0	0	0	0	0
8/20/98	CLE	3	2	1	0	0	1	1
8/21/98	NYA	4	0	2	0	0	0	0
8/22/98	NYA	4	2	2	0	0	2	5
8/23/98	NYA	4	1	1	0	0	0	1
8/24/98	DET	2	1	1	0	0	0	1
8/25/98	DET	4	1	1	1	0	0	1
8/26/98	DET	4	1	3	2	0	0	4
8/28/98	@ChA	5	1	1	0	0	1	2

Date	Opp	AB	R	H	2B	3B	HR	RBI
8/28/98	@ChA	5	0	2	0	0	0	0
8/29/98	@ChA	4	1	1	0	0	0	1
8/30/98	@ChA	4	0	1	0	0	0	0
8/31/98	@Det	5	3	4	2	1	1	7
9/01/98	@Det	4	0	1	0	0	0	1
9/02/98	@Det	5	1	2	0	0	0	0
9/04/98	MIN	4	1	2	1	0	0	2
9/05/98	MIN	5	1	2	0	0	1	1
9/06/98	MIN	4	0	3	1	0	0	1
9/07/98	MIN	4	1	2	0	0	1	1

Date	Opp	AB	R	H	2B	3B	HR	RBI
9/08/98	KC	4	0	2	0	0	0	0
9/09/98	KC	4	1	3	1	0	0	0
9/11/98	@TB	4	0	0	0	0	0	0
9/12/98	@TB	5	2	2	0	0	0	0
9/13/98	@TB	4	2	2	0	0	1	2
9/14/98	@Bal	4	0	2	1	0	0	0
9/15/98	@Bal	4	1	1	1	0	0	1
9/16/98	ANA	4	0	1	0	0	0	0
9/17/98	ANA	4	1	2	1	0	1	1
9/18/98	OAK	4	0	0	0	0	0	0

Date	Opp	AB	R	H	2B	3B	HR	RBI
9/19/98	OAK	4	1	2	0	0	1	1
9/20/98	OAK	4	0	0	0	0	0	0
9/21/98	@Ana	5	0	2	1	0	0	2
9/22/98	@Ana	3	1	2	1	0	1	1
9/23/98	@Ana	3	1	0	0	0	0	0
9/24/98	@Sea	5	1	2	2	0	0	0
9/25/98	@Sea	3	0	1	0	0	0	0
9/26/98	@Sea	3	1	1	1	0	0	0
9/27/98	@Sea	2	1	1	1	0	0	0
Totals		606	110	193	50	2	45	157

Ken Griffey, Jr.: The Home Run Kid

Author: Larry Stone
ISBN: 1-58261-041-x

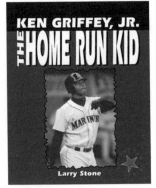

Capable of hitting majestic home runs, making breathtaking catches, and speeding around the bases to beat the tag by a split second, Ken Griffey, Jr. is baseball's Michael Jordan. Amazingly, Ken reached the Major Leagues at age 19, made his first All-Star team at 20, and produced his first 100 RBI season at 21.

The son of Ken Griffey, Sr., Ken is part of the only father-son combination to play in the same outfield together in the same game, and, like Barry Bonds, he's a famous son who turned out to be a better player than his father.

Sammy Sosa: Slammin' Sammy

Author: George Castle
ISBN: 1-58261-029-0

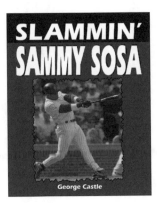

1998 was a break-out year for Sammy as he amassed 66 home runs, led the Chicago Cubs into the playoffs and finished the year with baseball's ultimate individual honor, MVP.

When the national spotlight was shone on Sammy during his home run chase with Mark McGwire, America got to see what a special person he is. His infectious good humor and kind heart have made him a role model across the country.

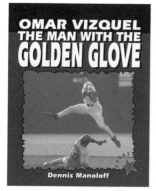

Omar Vizquel: The Man with the Golden Glove
Author: Dennis Manoloff
ISBN: 1-58261-045-2

Omar has a career fielding percentage of .982 which is the highest career fielding percentage for any shortstop with at least 1,000 games played.

Omar is a long way from his hometown of Caracas, Venezuela, but his talents as a shortstop put him at an even greater distance from his peers while he is on the field.

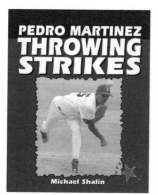

Pedro Martinez: Throwing Strikes
Author: Mike Shalin
ISBN: 1-58261-047-9

The 1997 National League Cy Young Award winner is always teased because of his boyish looks. He's sometimes mistaken for the batboy, but his curve ball and slider leave little doubt that he's one of the premier pitchers in the American League.

It is fitting that Martinez is pitching in Boston, where the passion for baseball runs as high as it does in his native Dominican Republic.

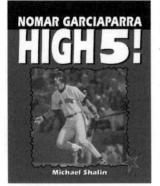

Nomar Garciaparra: High 5!
Author: Mike Shalin
ISBN: 1-58261-053-3

An All-American at Georgia Tech, a star on the 1992 U.S. Olympic Team, the twelfth overall pick in the 1994 draft, and the 1997 American League Rookie of the Year, Garciaparra has exemplified excellence on every level.

At shortstop, he'll glide deep into the hole, stab a sharply hit grounder, then throw out an opponent on the run. At the plate, he'll uncoil his body and deliver a clutch double or game-winning homer. Nomar is one of the game's most complete players.

Juan Gonzalez: Juan Gone!
Author: Evan Grant
ISBN: 1-58261-048-7

One of the most prodigious and feared sluggers in the major leagues, Gonzalez was a two-time home run king by the time he was 24 years old.

After having something of a personal crisis in 1996, the Puerto Rican redirected his priorities and now says baseball is the third most important thing in his life after God and family.

Sandy and Roberto Alomar:
Baseball Brothers

Author: Barry Bloom
ISBN: 1-58261-054-1

Sandy and Roberto Alomar are not just famous baseball brothers they are also famous baseball sons. Sandy Alomar, Sr. played in the major leagues fourteen seasons and later went into management. His two baseball sons have made names for themselves and have appeared in multiple All-Star games.

With Roberto joining Sandy in Cleveland, the Indians look to be a front-running contender in the American League Central.

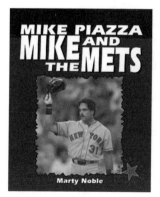

Mike Piazza:
Mike and the Mets

Author: Marty Noble
ISBN: 1-58261-051-7

A total of 1,389 players were selected ahead of Mike Piazza in the 1988 draft, who wasn't picked until the 62nd round, and then only because Tommy Lasorda urged the Dodgers to take him as a favor to his friend Vince Piazza, Mike's father.

Named in the same breath with great catchers of another era like Bench, Dickey and Berra, Mike has proved the validity of his father's constant reminder "If you work hard, dreams do come true."

Baseball
SuperStar Series Titles

Collect Them All!

_____ **Sandy and Roberto Alomar: Baseball Brothers**

_____ **Kevin Brown: Kevin with a "K"**

_____ **Roger Clemens: Rocket Man!**

_____ **Juan Gonzalez: Juan Gone!**

_____ **Mark Grace: Winning With Grace**

_____ **Ken Griffey, Jr.: The Home Run Kid**

_____ **Tony Gwynn: Mr. Padre**

_____ **Derek Jeter: The Yankee Kid**

_____ **Randy Johnson: Arizona Heat!**

_____ **Pedro Martinez: Throwing Strikes**

_____ **Mike Piazza: Mike and the Mets**

_____ **Alex Rodriguez: A-plus Shortstop**

_____ **Curt Schilling: Philly Phire!**

_____ **Sammy Sosa: Slammin' Sammy**

_____ **Mo Vaughn: Angel on a Mission**

_____ **Omar Vizquel: The Man with a Golden Glove**

_____ **Larry Walker: Colorado Hit Man!**

_____ **Bernie Williams: Quiet Superstar**

_____ **Mark McGwire: Mac Attack!**

Available by calling 877-424-BOOK

7920